In Touch With Nature
Mammals

BLACKBIRCH®
PRESS

THOMSON
———✳———
GALE

San Diego • Detroit • New York • San Francisco • Cleveland • New Haven, Conn. • Waterville, Maine • London • Munich

For more information, contact
The Gale Group, Inc.
27500 Drake Rd.
Farmington Hills, MI 48331-3535
Or you can visit our Internet site at http://www.gale.com

PHOTOGRAPHIC CREDITS
Corbis: Kit Houghton 16–17; **Photodisc:** 1, 4–5, 5t, 7t, 8–9, 10, 12, 15, 19, 20, 21, 22–23, 24, 26, 27.

Step-by-step photography throughout: Martin Norris

Front cover: Martin Norris and Photodisc

Consultant: Mark Hostetler, Ph.D.,
  Assistant Professor, Extension Wildlife Specialist,
  Department of Wildlife Ecology & Conservation,
  IFAS, University of Florida

For The Brown Reference Group plc
Editorial and Design: John Farndon and Angela Koo
Picture Researcher: Helen Simm
Illustrations: Darren Awuah
Managing Editor: Bridget Giles
Art Director: Dave Goodman
Children's Publisher: Anne O'Daly
Production Director: Alastair Gourlay
Editorial Director: Lindsey Lowe

LIBRARY OF CONGRESS CATALOGING-IN-PUBLICATION DATA

Available from the Library of Congress.

ISBN: 1-4103-0119-2

Printed and bound in Singapore
10 9 8 7 6 5 4 3 2 1

Contents

What are mammals?

Did you know?
The world's tallest land animal is the giraffe. It grows to more than 16 feet (5 m) tall.

Mammals are particular types of animals. They come in all shapes and sizes, from the tiny Etruscan shrew, a mouselike creature barely bigger than a person's thumb, to gigantic blue whales, which live in the ocean. Many familiar animals are mammals, including dogs, cats, cows, pigs, and horses. In fact, humans are mammals.

Like fish, birds, amphibians, and reptiles, mammals are vertebrates, or animals with backbones. The backbone is the main part of a skeleton of bones inside the body. The skeleton makes a strong frame that supports things such as muscles and skin. Mammals usually have two pairs of limbs. They have a skull that holds their brain, eyes, ears, and nose. They also have a heart, lungs, and guts inside their chest and abdomen.

Fox fur
Like many mammals, foxes have a coat of fur to keep them warm when it is cold—and cooler when it is hot.

4

CLOSE-UP *The largest mammals*

The biggest mammals are whales, which live in the sea. All whales are big, but the blue whale is huge. An average blue whale is more than 100 feet (30 m) long and weighs 90 tons (80 metric tons). To keep warm, whales do not have fur but a thick layer of fat called blubber. They are true mammals, though, and cannot breathe underwater like fish. Every minute or so—half an hour at the most—they come up to the surface to breathe air. Some whales, such as killer whales, have teeth. Others, like the humpback, have sieves called baleens in their mouth. They use the baleens to strain shrimp-like creatures called krill from the water to eat.

Killer whales are fearsome hunters. They feed on seals, porpoises, and penguins as well as fish.

Mammals are warm-blooded. Cold-blooded animals such as reptiles have to lie in the sun to warm up. Mammals, by contrast, make their own body heat. Most mammals are covered in fur, too. Their fur keeps the chill out when it is cold and keeps the heat out when it is hot. That means mammals can live just about anywhere. Meerkats live in the hottest parts of Africa. Polar bears live in the icy Arctic.

Mammal babies

Another thing that makes mammals different is the way they bring their young into the world. Nearly all mammals give birth to babies, rather than laying eggs as birds and most reptiles do. Once born, the babies feed on milk from their mother's teats.

Did you know?

Dolphins are really a kind of whale, and the biggest kind of dolphin is a killer whale.

Warm blood

Because mammals have warm blood, scientists say they are "endothermic." This means "warm inside." Mammals keep their bodies warm by eating lots of food. Food is fuel for the body, just as logs are fuel for a fire. Most mammals not only keep their bodies warm, they keep the same temperature all the time—between 97 °F (36 °C) and 102 °F (39 °C). To keep this steady temperature, a mammal's body must have ways to keep warm if things get cold. It must also have ways to keep cool if things get hot. Some mammals, including humans, sweat to keep cool. See if you can think of other ways mammals keep warm or cool. There is a list of some ways on page 7.

Rabbit fur
To stay equally warm all the time, mammals such as rabbits grow extra thick fur in winter. They then shed it in spring, which leaves a new thin coat for summer.

Did you know?
Unlike most mammals, bats cannot keep a steady temperature. They get cold when they sleep.

A STEADY TEMPERATURE

You will need:

✔ A tray of ice cubes, straight from the freezer

✔ A clinical thermometer from a pharmacist. This is used to test your body temperature when you are ill. Here, we have used one that goes underneath the tongue.

1 See how steady a mammal keeps its body warmth by checking your temperature with a thermometer under your tongue, once a day, for a week. It should always read 98.6 °F (36.9 °C).

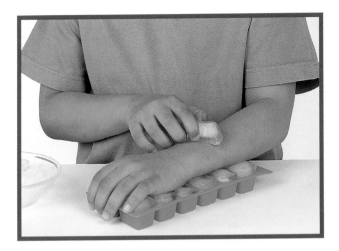

2 Put ice on your bare arm for a while, then look at the skin. You might see tiny bumps making the arm hairs stand up. All mammal hairs stand up like this to trap extra warm air when it is cold. Humans have so little hair, it does not help much, but it helps furry animals.

3 Stroke a pet mammal, like a cat or rabbit. Its fur feels warm because it is warmed by the animal's body heat. Now find a bare patch of skin, like inside the ears. Escaping body heat makes this area feel even warmer. If all its body was bare, the animal would lose too much heat and get cold.

Elephants flap their great big ears to help keep themselves cool.

A big mammal's body has a small surface area for its size. So it loses body heat slowly. A small mammal's body has a large surface area for its size, so it loses heat rapidly. To stay warm, a small mammal has to eat almost nonstop. Big animals do not have to eat as often. An elephant's problem is not keeping warm but staying cool in the tropical heat. An elephant has three ways to get cool. It loses heat by flapping its huge ears to cool the blood in them. It wallows in cool mud. And the wrinkles in its skin give it a bigger surface area to lose heat.

Ways to stay cool
* sweat—water oozes from skin pores and cools as it evaporates
* send more blood to the skin to cool off in the breeze
* lick—cats wet their fur
* pant—dogs cannot sweat, but blow over their tongue to cool off
* molt—mammals grow thinner fur to stay cool

Ways to keep warm
* stop sweating, panting, or licking
* keep blood away from the skin so it is not chilled by the wind
* shiver to work the muscles to make heat
* shelter or curl up out of the cold
* grow thick fur or add a layer of fat to keep out the cold

What mammals eat

Did you know?
Squirrel monkeys have more brain devoted to analyzing the sounds they hear than any other monkey or ape.

Mammals depend on other living things for their food. Some, called herbivores, eat mainly plants. Others, called carnivores, eat mostly meat by feeding on other animals.

Some herbivorous mammals are choosy. The koala eats only the leaves of 12 kinds of eucalyptus. Others eat a range of plants. Plant food is tough, so herbivores have strong teeth. Even so, teeth can wear down. Rodents such as rats have incisors (front teeth) that keep growing as they wear down.

Grazers and browsers

Some large herbivores, such as horses and buffalo, graze. This means they eat mainly grass. Browsers, including deer and antelope, eat the leaves, bark, and buds of bushes and trees. Small herbivores such as mice scurry to find seeds and grain. Monkeys climb trees to look mostly for fruit and nuts.

CLOSE-UP *Lions: large meat eaters*

Lions are among the largest carnivores. They can eat more than 75 pounds (34 kg) of meat in one meal! They usually gorge on a meal for a few hours, then rest for a few days. Lions hunt anything from baboons to hippos. But their favorite foods are medium-sized hoofed animals such as wildebeest, zebras, and antelopes. Lions mostly kill their own food, but they may steal the kills of other animals.

ON THE TRACK *Identifying droppings*

You can often tell by the droppings it leaves whether an animal is an herbivore or a meat eater.

1. If the dropping is a single sausage shape with bits of fur or feather, it is from a meat eater. This is a fox's dropping.

2. Lots of small round droppings are left by herbivores such as rabbits or sheep. These are a red deer's.

3. Badger droppings are a little like a fox's. But foxes go on open ground. Badgers go in a little pit they dig.

4. Moles are among the few insectivores with droppings big enough to see—about an inch long, gray, and studded with insect remains.

Animal eaters

Some meat-eating mammals, such as hyenas, eat carrion (meat left by others), but most hunt and kill animals themselves. They have keen senses to find their prey, strong agile bodies to catch it, and sharp teeth and claws to kill it. Meat is very nourishing compared to plants. So, while herbivores eat most of the time, carnivores rest after a meal, and save energy for the next hunt.

The biggest carnivores are cats such as lions and leopards, dogs such as wolves and foxes, and bears. Smaller carnivores include raccoons and mustelids, which are animals like martens and weasels.

Insectivores are small mammals such as shrews that eat insects. They eat other creatures, too, but they are not big hunters. Most mammals eat both plants and animals sometimes. But only animals like monkeys, apes, and humans are true omnivores. Omnivores are animals that eat both plants and animals most of the time.

Amazon squirrel monkey
These monkeys live in rainforest treetops. They feed on insects, fruit, and the sugary nectar of flowers.

Food power

Mammals get all the energy they need to keep warm and to move around from the food they eat. Like fuels such as gas, food contains energy in chemical form. Inside a mammal's body, foods are broken down into the right form to burn in the millions of tiny cells that make up the body. Of course, there are no flames when a mammal's body cells burn food fuel. There is just a chemical change. But energy and warmth are released just as in a fire. This experiment shows how real the energy in food is. Some foods are very high in energy; some are less so. Foods rich in chemicals called carbohydrates, like sugar and starch, usually contain the most energy.

Bear necessities
Grizzly bears spend most of their lives searching for food. They live mainly on plants such as berries. But they also catch fish and rodents, and even ants.

Alternative chimney (inset)
If you are using a large can instead, turn the can so the open end is downward. Then put four balls of modeling clay around the rim. This will allow air in underneath.

PEANUT ENERGY

You will need:

✔ Unsalted peanuts
✔ A coffee-pot holder or large can*
✔ A lighter or matches
✔ A small ringpull can
✔ Foil

✔ Scissors
✔ A jar with lid
✔ A cooking thermometer
✔ Water
✔ Tape

* The coffee-pot holder is used as a chimney. If you do not have a pot like this, a large empty can will do as well. Follow only the inset in Step 1 (top), then go straight to Step 2.

1 Wrap foil around the coffee-pot holder on either side of the handle. Tape the edges together to form a tube. Fold the ends of the tube neatly. Cut two small slots in the foil near the top of the pot.

2 Fill a clean, empty ringpull can with water. Measure its temperature with a cooking thermometer. Now place a peanut on the lid of the small jar.

3 With the help of an adult, light the peanut with a match or lighter. Then slot the coffee-pot holder or large can over the lit peanut with the base uppermost. Now rest the small can of water on top, on the base of the coffee-pot holder (inset far right). Once the peanut burns out, test the temperature of the water in the can. The water should now be much warmer, showing the peanut has given real heat energy.

CLOSE-UP
A healthy diet

Wild animals know by instinct what to eat. But pet owners must take care to give their pets the right food.

For a mammal's body to stay healthy, it must eat the right food. A mammal eats mostly for energy. Energy in food comes mainly from substances called carbohydrates and fats. More than 80 percent of energy food is used simply to keep warm. But a mammal must also eat foods such as proteins, which are needed to make and repair body cells. It must also eat tiny traces of chemicals called vitamins and minerals its body cannot make for itself. A healthful diet contains just the right mix.

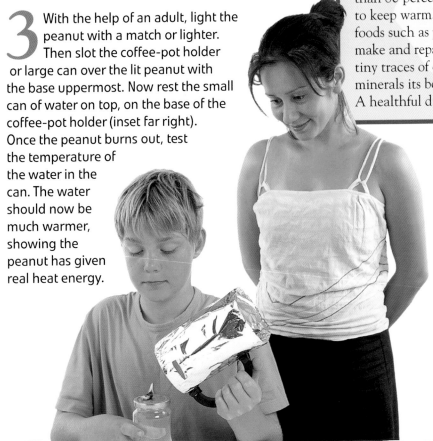

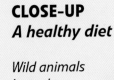

The pot is set up like this while the peanut burns.

Take care
Make sure you have an adult to help you with this experiment.

Mammal parents

Did you know?
If all the offspring of one pair of rabbits survived to breed, there would be 33 million rabbits in 3 years.

All mammals begin life as an egg inside their mother's body. But only a few, the monotremes, lay eggs like a bird. The Australian duck-billed platypus is a monotreme.

Many other Australian mammals, such as kangaroos and koalas, are marsupials. So is the American opossum. Marsupials have a pouch on their abdomens for their young.

A marsupial baby is tiny when it is born and cannot survive in the open. After it is born, it crawls into its mother's pouch and stays there until big enough to survive outside.

Most mammals, however, stay inside their mother's body until they are fully developed. Inside the mother's body is a chamber called the uterus, where the developing baby is nourished by food carried in the mother's

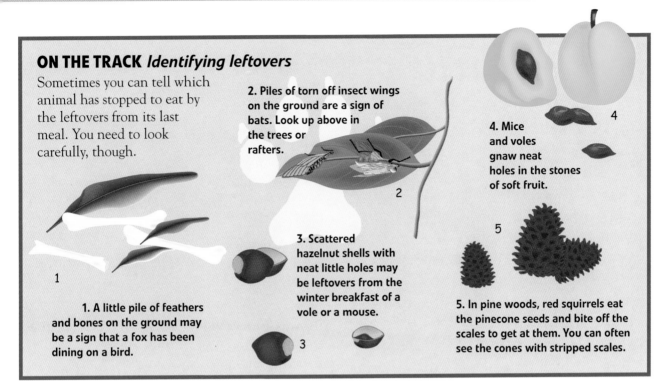

ON THE TRACK *Identifying leftovers*

Sometimes you can tell which animal has stopped to eat by the leftovers from its last meal. You need to look carefully, though.

1. A little pile of feathers and bones on the ground may be a sign that a fox has been dining on a bird.

2. Piles of torn off insect wings on the ground are a sign of bats. Look up above in the trees or rafters.

3. Scattered hazelnut shells with neat little holes may be leftovers from the winter breakfast of a vole or a mouse.

4. Mice and voles gnaw neat holes in the stones of soft fruit.

5. In pine woods, red squirrels eat the pinecone seeds and bite off the scales to get at them. You can often see the cones with stripped scales.

blood. These mammals are all called "placental" mammals because in the uterus the young are fed through an organ called the placenta. The placenta provides all the food needed for the baby to grow. Babies are not born until they are developed enough to survive in the open air.

Time to be born

Mammals create babies sexually. That means the mother only becomes pregnant after she has mated with a male. This usually only happens when the female is in a condition called estrus, or heat. Some mammals are in heat only at certain times of year. Others come into heat at any time.

The time between mating and birth is called the gestation period, or pregnancy. It varies from animal to animal. Bigger

animals usually have longer gestation periods and fewer babies than small ones.

Rabbits are born just a month after mating, and seven or eight baby rabbits may be born at once. African elephants are pregnant for at least 22 months, longer than any other animal. Elephants rarely have more than one calf. Horses have a gestation period of 11 months. Human gestation lasts about nine months.

CLOSE-UP *Mother's milk*

Mammals are the only animals to feed their young with milk. It is perfect food: nourishing, warm, and full of substances that help protect the young from disease. When a mammal gets pregnant, she starts to produce milk at teats on her chest, or under her body. The number of teats the mother has depends partly on the typical number of babies she has. Human mothers rarely have more than two babies, so they have just two teats. Mother pigs have lots of babies and have seven pairs of teats.

Lion cub and mother
For the first seven months of its life, a lion cub is looked after by its mother and feeds on her milk.

Breathing air

All mammals, including humans, must breathe to stay alive. When a mammal breathes in, it takes air into its body. Air contains the oxygen vital to the animal's every cell. Without oxygen, cells die instantly. This is why most mammals die if they stop breathing even for a few minutes. Just as fire needs air to burn, body cells need oxygen to burn their chemical food. Blood carries food to body cells as glucose, an energy-rich chemical. When a cell burns glucose to unlock its energy, some of the glucose is turned into a gas called carbon dioxide. Carbon dioxide is poisonous, so a mammal gets rid of it when breathing out. The first experiment here shows how the air you breathe out is rich in carbon dioxide.

BREATH TESTS

You will need:
- ✔ Pickling lime (used for tortillas and pickling)
- ✔ Drinking straw
- ✔ Large screwtop jar; small jar
- ✔ Length of plastic tube
- ✔ Large bowl
- ✔ Marker pen

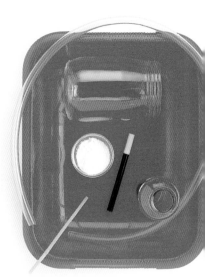

Did you know?
If you live to the age of 75, you will take about 600 million breaths in your lifetime.

1 Add a few spoonfuls of lime to a jar of tap water to make limewater. Breathe gently into the water through a straw. At first, the limewater is clear, then tiny specks of chalk begin to appear.

2 The chalk specks are made by carbon dioxide in your breath reacting with the limewater. As more chalk is made, the water turns white. This shows your breath contains carbon dioxide.

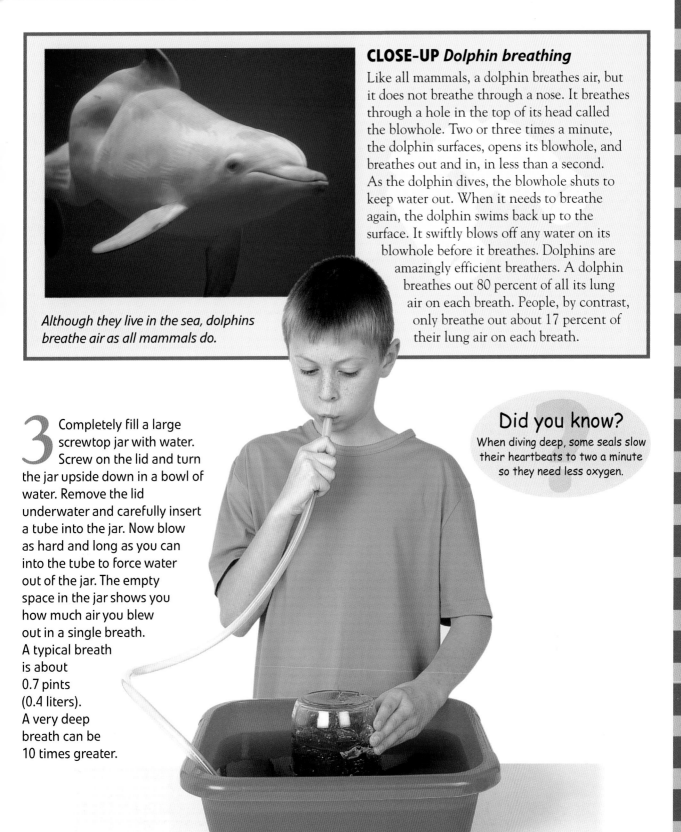

CLOSE-UP *Dolphin breathing*

Like all mammals, a dolphin breathes air, but it does not breathe through a nose. It breathes through a hole in the top of its head called the blowhole. Two or three times a minute, the dolphin surfaces, opens its blowhole, and breathes out and in, in less than a second. As the dolphin dives, the blowhole shuts to keep water out. When it needs to breathe again, the dolphin swims back up to the surface. It swiftly blows off any water on its blowhole before it breathes. Dolphins are amazingly efficient breathers. A dolphin breathes out 80 percent of all its lung air on each breath. People, by contrast, only breathe out about 17 percent of their lung air on each breath.

Although they live in the sea, dolphins breathe air as all mammals do.

3 Completely fill a large screwtop jar with water. Screw on the lid and turn the jar upside down in a bowl of water. Remove the lid underwater and carefully insert a tube into the jar. Now blow as hard and long as you can into the tube to force water out of the jar. The empty space in the jar shows you how much air you blew out in a single breath. A typical breath is about 0.7 pints (0.4 liters). A very deep breath can be 10 times greater.

Did you know?
When diving deep, some seals slow their heartbeats to two a minute so they need less oxygen.

Mammals on the move

Mammals move in many different ways, but most live on the ground and move on four legs. Reptiles, such as lizards, move on four legs, too. But a mammal's legs move backward and forward under its body, while a reptile's are bent out to the side. So mammals can move farther and faster than reptiles.

Walking, trotting, and galloping

When four-legged mammals want to move slowly, they walk. To walk, they put one foot forward at a time. To go a little faster, they trot—lift one front foot and the opposite back foot together. Dogs, cats, and hoofed animals do this even when moving slowly. A few animals, such as giraffes, pace rather than trot. To pace, they move both left feet, then both right feet. To go really fast, four-legged mammals gallop. A gallop is really a succession of leaps, with both back feet or front feet landing almost together.

CLOSE-UP *Horses and hooves*

Horses belong to a mammal group called ungulates, which also includes antelopes, deer, and rhinos. Ungulates live in wide-open grasslands and feed on grass. There are few hiding places in grasslands, and horses and other ungulates rely on speed to escape from predators. They have long legs for running. Ungulates also have special hard toes called hooves. Hooves enable horses to run very fast on the tips of their toes, without their heels even touching the ground.

ON THE TRACK *Identifying animal hair*

Animals leave hairs on barbed-wire fences. Hairs at the top of the fence may be from cows, horses, or deer. Hairs lower down may be from badgers, rabbits, or foxes.

2

4

2. Cow hairs are short, soft, and matted like felt.

4. Horse hairs are long and stiff.

3

1

5

1. Rabbit hairs are 0.5 inches (10–15 mm) long, fine, soft, and fluffy.

3. Badger hairs are 2–3 inches (50–75 mm) long, wiry, and black and white.

5. Fox hairs are 1 inch (25 mm) long, straight, and red and brown.

Hopping, climbing, and flying

Rabbits have especially strong back legs and tend to hop, not walk. A few mammals, such as kangaroos, have such huge hind feet that they never go down on all fours. Instead, they hop everywhere and use their tails for balance. Some mammals are good tree climbers. Monkeys have long arms for swinging and hands and feet for grasping branches.

A few mammals, such as American monkeys and opossums, also have a prehensile tail. That is a tail that can grip. Squirrels and sloths have sharp, curved claws for hooking into bark like a grappling iron. Flying foxes have webs of skin between their legs so they can glide huge distances between trees. Bats have wings and can fly.

Did you know?
Red kangaroos can leap 20 feet (6 m) straight up in the air.

Mammal senses

Most mammals have five major senses to tell them what is going on around them: sight, sound, smell, taste, and touch. But some senses are far stronger in certain animals than others. Most mammals, for instance, have a much better sense of smell than humans, apes, and monkeys. They find food mainly by sniffing it out. Many mammals have sharper hearing than humans, too. Bats and dolphins have hearing so sharp that they can use it to find their way. But eyesight is important for nearly all mammals. Having two eyes is also crucial for judging how far away things are, as this experiment shows. Humans are especially good at this.

JUDGING DISTANCE

You will need:

✔ **Modeling clay**
✔ **Target (this can simply be a plate or a mark on the floor)**
✔ **Notebook and pen**
✔ **Treats or ball for dog to catch**
✔ **Ruler**

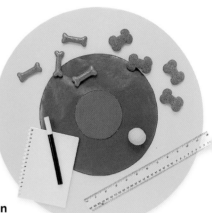

Did you know?

Whales can sense Earth's magnetic field. They use it to find their way.

1 Create a target on the floor, then sit about 10 feet (3 m) away. Get a friend to hold a ball of modeling clay over the target. Give him or her instructions so they drop the ball on the target.

2 Repeat ten times. Measure how far from the center of the target the ball lands each time. Find the average distance from the target by adding all the distances together and dividing by ten.

3 Now place your hand over one eye and repeat steps 1 and 2. Try the same with the other eye. You will find you are not as accurate on average with one eye as with two. One of your eyes alone may also be worse than the other.

Seeing in depth

Herbivores such as horses have eyes that face sideways. This lets them spot a predator coming from any direction. But their judgment of distance can be poor. Humans and most hunting mammals have eyes that face forward and can judge distances very well. Each eye gives a different view, and the views combine in the brain to give an idea of depth (how far away a thing is). This is called binocular vision. Try throwing a ball or treat to a dog. Binocular vision helps a pet dog judge its leap to catch a ball— and a wild dog to pounce on prey.

CLOSE-UP *Night vision*

The slow loris of Asia has huge round eyes that narrow to a slit in the day, then open wide in the dark to give keen night vision.

All mammals can see a little at night. Mammal eyes have a round window called the pupil, which opens wider in the dark to allow more light in. But animals that are active at night, including cats, can open their pupils much wider. That means they can see very well in the dark. Bobcats can see six times better than humans can at night! Animals that are entirely nocturnal also have an organ in the eye called the tapetum. This reflects light back into the eye, so the eye's detectors get a second chance to pick the light up. It is the tapetum that makes the eyes of animals such as foxes shine in the headlights of a car.

Did you know?

Rats and mice see well at night, partly because they can see ultraviolet light that is invisible to humans.

Attack and defense

Did you know?
An African antelope called a springbok can jump 10 feet (3 m) straight up when alarmed.

Sometimes a mammal is chased by a predator—another animal that wants to kill and eat it. When this happens, many mammals try to escape by running away. Hoofed animals such as antelopes can run far and fast. Other animals, such as rabbits and baby deer, stay still because many predators only see their prey when it moves. The American opossum plays dead!

Many mammals try to avoid being seen in the first place. They come out at night when predators cannot see well, or during the day, when night-hunting predators are not about. All kinds of small mammals, such as prairie dogs, dig burrows they can sleep in at night or run to when danger threatens.

Colored for safety

Most mammals boost their survival chances by growing coats to blend in with the color of their surroundings. This makes them harder to see. Animal experts call this "protective coloration." Most mammals are brownish, making them hard to see against bare ground and tree trunks. Arctic hares and other mammals that live where there is lots of snow turn white in winter. Their coats change back to brown in the summer.

Another way a mammal fools a predator's eyes is with "disruptive coloration"—when an animal's coat is so strongly patterned it is hard to see the animal's overall shape. The striking stripes of zebras work like this.

CLOSE-UP *Porcupine weapons*

Few mammals have any defenses besides kicking, biting, and scratching. Some, like antelopes, have sharp horns. Armadillos are protected by armor. Hedgehogs are covered in short spines. Porcupines have something extra. Porcupines move so slowly they cannot escape by running. But their backs are covered in long, needle-sharp spines called quills. Any predator that tries to bite into a porcupine gets a nasty mouthful of spikes. The quills come away easily, and their tips are barbed. The unfortunate attacker will find the quills painfully embedded in its skin and hard to shake out. The porcupine can afford to lose a quill or two. The North American porcupine has more than 30,000 on its back!

The North American porcupine is the largest porcupine. It lives in woods in the north and west of North America.

Stripe confusion
A Bengal tiger's stripes break its outline and make it much harder to see as it stalks through the grass hunting for prey.

The last defense

If a predator catches up, many insects and reptiles such as snakes defend themselves with poison. No mammals do. Skunks and their relatives spray a foul-smelling liquid when threatened, but that is the closest mammals get to chemical warfare. Instead, they rely mostly on kicking, biting, and scratching. Many mammals, including buffalo, herd together to protect themselves by sheer weight of numbers.

Mammal killers

Hunting mammals rely on speed, strength, and cunning to catch their victims. Solitary hunters such as tigers and leopards stalk their prey with stealth before pouncing. Mammals that hunt in groups, such as wolves, take turns chasing their prey, until the prey is worn out. Once caught, the victim is killed with sharp teeth and claws.

Did you know?
If a wood mouse is caught by its tail, it quickly sheds the end to escape.

Mammals through the year

Did you know?
Macaque monkeys in Japan stay warm in winter by taking baths in hot volcanic springs.

With their warm bodies and insulating fur, mammals are very good at coping with changing weather. But even mammals have to adapt to the changing of the seasons, because their food supply varies. Many mammals have their babies in spring, for instance. That means the babies can grow up in the summer, when food is plentiful.

In many places, there is a time of year when plant food is scarce. In tropical grasslands, this is the dry season. Every May in east Africa, the rains stop and the land dries up. Vast herds of wildebeest, zebras, and antelopes move in search of grass and water. Lions and other hunting animals that feed on them follow. When the rains come again and fresh grass springs up, the herds return. On this yearly journey, the animals travel more than 1,500 miles (2,400 km).

Yearly journeys like this are called migrations. In cool regions, winter is

Winter trek
In winter, moose migrate south to places, such as Wyoming, where there is more food and water under the snow than in the northern tundra.

Did you know?
By slowing their hearts from 400 beats a minute to 14, bats use hardly any energy when hibernating.

the time when food is scarce. Large grazing animals in these areas migrate, too. In North America, herds of caribou travel south from the open tundra in the far north to forests where they spend the winter.

Toughing it out

Many mammals are too small to migrate large distances. They must stay put and cope with the changing weather. Some, such as squirrels, mice, and beavers, build up a store of food in the fall to help them through the lean winter. Rabbits, deer, and others change their diet and live on the food that is available, even if it is only moss and bark.

Many small mammals survive the winter by becoming less active, so they do not need so much food. Some fatten themselves up in fall, then go into a kind of sleep called hibernation. During hibernation, body processes slow down. For some animals, like raccoons, this sleep is light. Others sleep so deeply they look dead. Body temperatures can drop below 6 °F (–14 °C) and heart rates slow to 10 beats a minute. Hibernators do not stay asleep all winter, but wake from time to time. Most small mammals hibernate in burrows and holes safe from predators. Bears do not really hibernate. They doze for months in their dens.

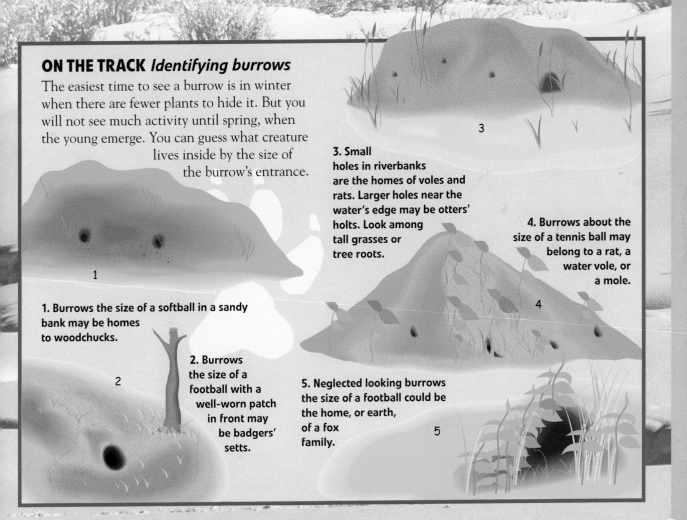

ON THE TRACK *Identifying burrows*

The easiest time to see a burrow is in winter when there are fewer plants to hide it. But you will not see much activity until spring, when the young emerge. You can guess what creature lives inside by the size of the burrow's entrance.

3. Small holes in riverbanks are the homes of voles and rats. Larger holes near the water's edge may be otters' holts. Look among tall grasses or tree roots.

4. Burrows about the size of a tennis ball may belong to a rat, a water vole, or a mole.

1. Burrows the size of a softball in a sandy bank may be homes to woodchucks.

2. Burrows the size of a football with a well-worn patch in front may be badgers' setts.

5. Neglected looking burrows the size of a football could be the home, or earth, of a fox family.

Mammal tracks

Most wild mammals are shy and hard to see. But you can often tell where they have been from the tracks they leave behind. In winter, tracks in snow are often easy to see. In summer, look in mud beside creeks and marshes, on sandy beaches, or in the soft earth of woodland floors and gardens. Frequently used paths or game trails are also good places to look. Look, too, along the edge of a wood, or along the banks of a stream. If you know a place where animals often go, then you can prepare a smooth patch of ground for their tracks by sweeping with a tree branch. If you find a good track, you can preserve it forever in the way shown here.

Fox on the prowl
Like all dogs, foxes leave tracks with four toes and a pad at the back. This makes it hard to tell a fox's track from a pet dog's.

PRESERVING ANIMAL TRACKS

You will need:

✔ Animal tracks found in mud or sand
✔ Measuring jar
✔ Mixing bowl
✔ Plaster of Paris
✔ Water
✔ Sticky tape
✔ Card
✔ Scissors
✔ Spoon

1 Clear away any loose soil or leaves around the tracks. Then choose the best-looking track print. Tape the card into a ring shape and press it firmly down into the mud or sand around the print.

2 Mix the plaster of Paris with water in the bowl. Pour and spoon the mixture into the ring and smooth it down.

3 When the plaster is set, carefully lift away the mold in its cardboard. Leave it for a day to harden completely, then remove the card and brush away the dirt.

Observation
Preserving animal tracks is a good way to get to know them. It is also a good way of keeping a record of which animals have moved through a particular area.

ON THE TRACK *Identifying tracks*

One way to identify tracks is to look at the number of toes on each foot. Four toes on each foot suggests a kind of dog (such as a fox), cat, or rabbit. Four on the front and five on the back is a rodent (like voles or mice). Five toes on each foot may be a kind of raccoon, or a badger, mink, otter, skunk, or opossum. Two-toe tracks could be deer or moose. Signs of hopping, with large hind feet landing in front of small forefeet, suggest a squirrel or rabbit.

front / rear / front / rear / front / rear

gray wolf   **cottontail rabbit**   **beaver**

red fox   **white-tailed deer**   rear / front   **weasel**

rear / front   rear / front

front / rear   rear / front

meadow vole   **squirrel**   **deer mouse**

Did you know?
A snowshoe hare's big footprints spread the hare's scent out, making it hard for predators to follow.

Where mammals live

Did you know?
Arctic foxes can survive nights on open ice floes with temperatures below -90.4 °F (-68 °C).

Mammals are very adaptable creatures, but they each have their own preferred place to live, or habitat. And every major habitat, from deep oceans to bone-dry deserts, has its own particular mammals. Grasslands and woodlands are home to very different creatures, for example. Grasslands in cool parts of the world may be home to vast herds of grazing mammals, such as the buffalo that once roamed North America's prairies before hunters killed them in large numbers. Other grassland mammals include small animals such as prairie dogs and other rodents. To protect themselves from predators in summer and cold in winter, these animals live in burrows under the ground. They emerge only on summer days.

CLOSE-UP *Arctic survivors*

The Arctic is one of the harshest of all habitats. There is a brief summer when plants bloom and insects multiply on the fringes. But for half the year, it is bitterly cold and almost always dark. Yet a few mammals such as Arctic foxes and polar bears manage to survive here year-round. Foxes live on the edge and polar bears live right in the icy heart of the Arctic. Polar bears have very thick fur and a layer of blubber to keep out the cold. In winter, females hibernate in dens. Males wander over the frozen sea and prey on seals. They catch the seals by waiting for them to come up for air through their breathing holes in the ice.

Polar bears can get food from beneath the Arctic ice, even in the depths of winter.

Woodlands are home to a wide range of creatures. In summer, leaves, fruit, nuts, and seeds are food for small mammals such as chipmunks and voles, and also for insects. The insects, in turn, are food for insect-eating mammals such as shrews and badgers. All of these small mammals are eaten by hunters such as weasels and foxes. Foxes and bears also wander the woods and forage for all kinds of food.

Tropical habitats

East African grasslands often have huge herds of large grass-eating animals. These include zebras and buffalo and many kinds of antelopes such as gazelles, impalas, and wildebeest. These grazers are hunted by big carnivores such as lions and cheetahs. There are also even bigger browsers such as hippos, rhinos, elephants, and giraffes.

Treetop feast
Squirrels make the most of woodlands. They feed on fruit and fungi in summer, nuts and acorns in winter.

Where grasslands turn to desert, with little water and extreme heat, life gets tough for mammals. But some can cope well. The addax, a large antelope of the Sahara, gets all its water from its food. Kangaroo rats in California's Death Valley save water by eating their own droppings. Desert foxes lose heat through their big ears. Some animals, such as ground squirrels, stay cool by sheltering in burrows.

Rain forests, too, are home to a unique range of mammals. Climbing animals such as monkeys, apes, and lemurs live up in the treetops. Down on the ground, large mammals such as tapirs and deer forage. They are hunted by carnivores such as leopards and jaguars.

Did you know?
Kit foxes have thick fur on their paws to keep them from being burned on scorching desert sand.

Identifying mammals

There are about 4,600 different species (kinds) of mammals. If you see one in the wild, you can begin to identify it by deciding what kind of animal it is: carnivore or herbivore, large or small. See if you can fit it into one of these groups by using the identification clues.

Mammals as large or larger than a dog*:

 Large carnivore: Looks like a cat or dog or bear, and has eyes facing forward.

 Large grazer or browser: Hooves on its feet, eyes on the side of its head, perhaps horns.

Mammals smaller than a dog:

 Small carnivore: Long and thin with long, bushy tail, and short legs.

 Opossum: Lives in trees and has long bare tail, very big ears, and long soft snout.

 Rodent: Much smaller than a dog, with two very sharp front teeth.

 Insectivore: Very small and velvety and without two sharp front teeth.

Flying mammals:

 Bat: You can tell a bat from a bird instantly, because it has no feathers or tail.

There are also the mammals that live in the sea, including whales and seals.

A dog the size of a labrador or other retriever.

LARGE CARNIVORES

Large carnivores are either a kind of dog, a kind of cat, or a kind of bear.

ID clues:
- Dogs have a long snout and long, thin legs.
- Cats have a short face and strong legs.
- Bears have big, barrel-shaped bodies and thick limbs with handlike forepaws.

Dogs and their relatives: Family CANIDAE
There are 36 species of dogs. They eat mostly meat and have long front teeth called canines for tearing prey. They also eat plants and insects. They are good runners and chase prey for long distances until it is exhausted. Wolves and others hunt in packs. Dogs, such as foxes, hunt alone.
Dogs include: *Wolves, foxes, coyotes*

Bears: Family URSIDAE
There are 9 species of bears. All but the spectacled bear live in the northern half of the world. Bears are the biggest carnivores. The Alaskan brown bear grows up to 9 feet (3 m) tall. Most bears have a very varied diet, including insects, grass, leaves, fruit, and nuts as well as fish and larger animals.
Bears include: *Grizzlies, black bears, polar bears*

Cats and their relatives: Family FELIDAE
There are 38 species of cats. They are all fast, agile hunters with strong legs for catching prey in brief chases or lightning-fast pounces. Their claws extend to grip the victim's flesh. But they kill prey with a strong and sudden bite.
Cats include: *Cougars, lynxes*

LARGE GRAZERS

Outside the tropics, large grazers are horses, deer, pronghorns, or bovids.

ID clues:

• Horses have a long snout with a round end and also a mane on their neck.

• Deer are slim and long-legged. Males have branching horns called antlers.

• Bovids all have two horns on their head.

• Pronghorns are like bovids with two horns, but each horn has a little extra spike.

Horses and their relatives: Family EQUIDAE
There are 10 species of horses, including zebras and asses, as well as the domestic horse. Scientists group the horse family with tropical rhinos and tapirs because they all have an even number of toes on each foot.
Horses include: *Mustangs, asses, donkeys*

Deer: Family CERVIDAE
There are 40 species of deers. Male deer have branching antlers of bone (not horn) that drop off and grow again each year. Most deer spend some of the year in or near woods and browse on bark and leaves. They also eat grass.
Deer include: *Elk, caribou, moose, white-tailed deer*

Bovids: Family BOVIDAE
There are 137 species of bovids. They are all related to farm cattle, but they vary enormously, from mountain goats to giant buffalo (bison). The family includes the huge number of agile antelopes that live on tropical grasslands.
Bovids include: *Buffalos, bighorn sheep, mountain goats, domestic cattle*

Pronghorn: Family ANTILOCAPRIDAE
There is only 1 species of pronghorn. It looks like a cross between an antelope and a deer, and can run at speeds of up to 40 mph (64 km/h).

SMALL CARNIVORES

Small carnivores are mustelids, or they belong to the raccoon or civet family.

ID clues:

• Mustelids nearly all have long, limber bodies, short legs, and long tails.

• Raccoons have a distinctive black and white "bandit" mask.

• The civet family only lives in the tropics.

Mustelids: Family MUSTELIDAE
There are 67 species in the mustelid or weasel family. They include weasels themselves, ferrets, and martens, and have slim bodies and short legs perfect for chasing prey down burrows. Badgers and big, bearlike wolverines are also mustelids.
Mustelids include: *Weasels, minks, ferrets, wolverines, badgers, otters*

Raccoons and their relatives: Family PROCYONIDAE
There are 18 species in the raccoon family. They are good climbers, with short legs and long bushy tails. Only the North American raccoon lives outside the tropics.
Raccoons include: *Raccoons, olingos, kinkajous*

OPOSSUMS

Opossums are marsupials. Only the Virginia opossum lives in North America.

ID clues:

• Opossums have a long, whiskered snout and big round ears that are pink inside.

• They have a furry body and a long bare tail.

• Opossums may sometimes "play possum" (pretend to be dead) if threatened.

RODENTS & RELATIVES

These could be from one of three animal groups: rabbits; rats and mice; or squirrels and beavers.

ID clues:

• Rabbits and their relatives have big eyes and ears, a round snout, and a short tail.

• Rats and mice have a pointed face with long whiskers and a long, thin, bare tail.

• Squirrels and their relatives usually have a bushy tail and can sit upright to hold their food in their front paws.

Rabbit relatives: The lagomorphs
There are 80 species of rabbits and their relatives. Although they have two incisors like rodents, scientists put them in a separate group because they have an extra upper pair of teeth to help them with their entirely vegetarian diet.
Rabbit relatives include: *Rabbits, hares, pikas*

Rat and mice relatives: The myomorphs
There are 1,137 species of mouselike rodents—a quarter of all mammals. They are mostly small, active only at night, and eat seeds. But brown rats eat almost anything and live almost anywhere.
Mouse relatives include: *Mice, rats, lemmings, muskrats, voles*

Squirrel relatives: The sciuromorphs
There are 377 species of squirrel-like rodents. They can be distinguished from myomorphs because they are generally bigger. They also have a wide range of lifestyles. Squirrels live in woods, beavers in streams, and prairie dogs under the prairies.
Squirrel relatives include: *Beavers, woodchucks, chipmunks, squirrels, ground squirrels, prairie dogs, gophers*

INSECTIVORES

Insectivores are likely to be moles, shrews or, in Europe and Asia, hedgehogs.

ID clues:

• Moles are small, velvety creatures with large front paws for digging and eyes so small they are virtually blind.

• Shrews are very tiny with a long, pointed snout and very small, pointed teeth.

• Hedgehogs are covered in spines like a scrubbing brush.

Shrews: Family SORICIDAE
There are 280 species of shrews. The world's smallest mammals are shrews. They all have very fast heartbeats (up 1,200 beats a minute) and have to eat constantly to keep up energy levels.
Shrews include: *Short-tailed shrews*

FLYING MAMMALS

Bats are the only mammals that can fly. A quarter of all mammal species are bats.

ID clues:

• Only experts can tell the difference between the different species of bats.

• If you see a small brown bat near streams, it is likely to be a little brown myotis.

• If you see bats roosting in buildings, they are likely to be big brown bats.

Evening bats: Family VESPERTILIONIDAE
There are 318 species of evening bats. Most fly out at dusk to hunt for flying insects, which they find by "echolocation." This involves listening for reflections of the high-pitched squeals they emit.
Evening bats include: *Little brown myotis, big brown bat, fish-eating bat*

Glossary

blubber A thick layer of fat that helps sea mammals such as whales and seals keep warm.

browser Plant-eating animal that feeds on the leaves, buds, and shoots of trees and bushes.

carbohydrates Foods made from kinds of sugar such as starch. Inside an animal's body, these are turned into a special kind of sugar that the animal's body cells can use as energy fuel.

carbon dioxide A waste gas expelled from the body when an animal breathes out.

carnivore Any animal that eats meat. It can also mean a mammal that hunts other animals.

carrion The flesh of a dead animal, often left over after it has been hunted and killed.

cell One of the millions of microscopically small packages that make up every living thing.

cellular respiration The process in which an animal's body cells release energy from sugar with the help of oxygen.

endothermic Describes a warm-blooded animal able to generate its own body heat.

fats Greasy foods that do not dissolve in water. They are a source of energy for mammals, but not as good as carbohydrates. In the body, fat is used to store energy.

gestation period The time it takes a young animal to develop inside its mother's body.

grazer Animal that eats mainly grass.

herbivore Animal that feeds mostly on plant matter such as grass and leaves.

hibernation A deep sleep that many animals go into in winter when food is hard to find. Body processes slow down to save energy.

insectivore Animal that eats mainly insects.

marsupial Animal whose young develop in a pouch on its mother's abdomen.

migration An animal's long seasonal journey to find food or to breed.

monotreme Mammal that lays eggs.

omnivore Animal that eats most foods.

oxygen The gas that all animals need to get energy from their food. Mammals must breathe in frequently to get oxygen from the air.

placenta Part of a mother mammal's body that supplies food and oxygen to the baby developing in her uterus.

predator Animal that lives by hunting others.

prey Animal hunted by a predator for food.

protein The main building material of living things. A mammal must include proteins in its diet to help keep its body healthy.

starch Energy-rich carbohydrate food found in the seeds, fruit, and other parts of plants.

sugar Sweet-tasting carbohydrates found in many plants and used by the body as an energy source. Table sugar is just one kind.

FURTHER READING:
John Grassy and Chuck Keene. National Audubon *First Field Guide: Mammals*. New York, NY: Scholastic, 1998.

John Farndon. *The Wildlife Atlas*. Pleasantville, NY: Reader's Digest, 2002.

John Farrand. National Audubon *Pocket Guide to Familiar Mammals of North America*. Westminster, MA: Alfred A. Knopf, 1993.

Steve Parker, Eyewitness Guide: *Mammal*. Westminster, MA: Alfred A. Knopf, 1989.

Index